Hail Sisters
of the Revolution

Caroline Gilfillan – Poems

Andrew Scott – Photographs

Published by Cowslip Press

Cowslip

9 Casson Street
Ulverston
LA12 7JQ

First Published in 2022

Cataloguing in Publication Data for this book is available from
the British Library.

ISBN 978 1 9996097 88

Designed and formatted by Russell Holden at Pixel Tweaks
www.pixeltweakspublications.com

Contents

Poems

The Women's Liberation Movement of the 1970s

Caroline Gilfillan

In 1974, when I moved to London along with the friends and fellow musicians who appear in these poems, the Women's Liberation Movement was growing apace. It needed to, because discrimination against women was prevalent in every aspect of society. We were sick of being patronised, belittled and ignored. Many of us had grown up in homes with mothers who, after finding respect and freedom during the Second World War, were then required to give up their jobs and status, and return to being wives and mothers in the 1950s. I believe some of that rubbed off on us.

This was a time of great flowering of women's talents, as they began to form women-only groups, so they could explore their own potential without having to fight against the dominance of men. Women's bands, artistic collectives, history groups, and campaigning groups were formed. Did we agree all the time? No. There were many fiery late-night discussions. But we were at the heart of these debates, and not sitting on the side-lines or making the tea.

This was a time for exploring sexuality, too. Many of us were in relationships with good, loving men, but the lamentable lack of knowledge about women's sexuality among both sexes often made those relationships frustrating. Some of us started to explore relationships with other women, and entered thrilling territory where a woman's sexual satisfaction was considered as important as that of a man. Women-only social events provided a welcome space where we could dance, flirt, chat and have fun, without the fear of being pestered – or worse – by men.

Meanwhile, as young women, we were addressing the nitty-gritty problems of making a living and finding homes. This was a time when big cities were still pock-marked by bomb sites, and rental properties scarce. As Andrew Scott explains in his introductory piece, in London a squatting movement was developing. I was one of many who occupied vacant properties, doing the necessary work to make them weather-proof and habitable. The squatting and housing unions also took on racist and bigoted landlords, starting the essential work of demanding safe, affordable housing for all – an aim that is sadly still distant in the 21st century.

It was a time of huge change. I'm glad I was a part of it.

Squatting in the 1970s

Andrew Scott

As a new arrival in London finding a place to live that offered some security was very difficult in the mid 1970s. Private rented places were relatively inexpensive but with rent controls and security for tenants these places were thin on the ground. I remember going to a couple of places with rooms to let and joining queues of other hopefuls as the tenant gave us the once over. How they decided who to pick was a mystery. I remember bumping into a guy I'd met at one of these gatherings. He was convinced he was going to be successful as he had advised the tenant how to fix her leaking bath tap. Or something.

Council housing made up a large part of the housing in London, particularly in the inner East End where council estates provided the majority of homes. No 'right to buy' in those days. But waiting lists were long and councils had no obligation to house single people. Councils also owned a lot of properties they'd bought, sometimes to renovate, often to demolish, to make way for new estates of council flats, or schools and parks, but didn't have the money to do any of these things. The houses, nearly always houses, sat empty, often for years. So 'problem meet solution'.

Squatting was not for the faint hearted. 'Breaking and entering' a property, even a semi-derelict house, was a criminal offence. The places were usually in poor condition and often had no bathrooms or inside toilets. But actually living in a squat was not illegal. If the owner wanted you out it was a civil matter, not a criminal one. The trick was to find a place that the landlord was in no hurry to re-possess. Local knowledge was precious. Through contacts with the squatting community in an area places could be found which were 'squattable'. And with energy and shared know-how the houses could be repaired, services connected, coin-operated phones installed.

I was staying in a flat in a converted Georgian town house in Pimlico. This, courtesy of a guy I knew who had an arrangement with the developer to let him live in the place until they found a buyer. After many fruitless weeks searching for somewhere more permanent Caroline came round one day and asked me if I wanted to join her and a few friends in a squat in Stepney. They had been evicted from Stoneyard Lane and were now squatting a house in York Square. The best news I'd had since moving to London.

Hail Sisters of the Revolution

Our mothers welded rivets, tightened nuts.
They slammed bomb shelter doors shut,
folded bank notes into their own wallets.

But in dingy peace time they got chopped down
to size, squashed into kitchens, hobbled
until their feet left bloody tracks on the tiles.

In our denim-jacket pockets, between the pages
of *Our Bodies, Ourselves*, we carried their
screwed-up hopes, their rage,
and on International Women's Day

traipsed to the bus stop on Commercial Road,
and joined the rowdy shuffle heading for
Trafalgar Square, arms linked, singing,

*The Women's Army is marching, Oh sisters
don't you weep.* Later we danced in DMs to
Young Hearts Run Free, downed pints of bitter,

held shy hands and snogged in corners.
Held each other in sheets that had never seen
an iron, hearts beating loud as snare drums.

We formed a band

As girl singers in a soul band
we'd clipped braces on to hot pants,
stumbled on stage in high-heeled clogs,
stacking our harmonies like beer-mats
on a sopping bar, ringing the chimes
on tambourines flecked with blood

while the boys in the band
loosed rough and thump,
twang and strut,
                    which *we* wanted some of,

so when we landed in London we blagged
some gear, learned how to play, and scrambled
out of the girl-singer nest, fluttering until our feathers
grew long and sombre and lifted us
onto soot-speckled roofs
                    where we perched

beside the chimney stacks, feeding on smoke
and sisterhood, hurling songs like buckets of tar
on to starers, swaggerers, wolf whistlers.

Gig

Five flights of stairs and still we climb carrying those speakers
the size of restaurant wheelie-bins.

Then it's cannon plug into mixer, jack into socket, hot frizzle
         of dust frying on valves,
dimpled snare-drum skin, misted metal of rims and screws,
splintered drum sticks, buzz-hum shaking speaker cloth.

Afterwards, unplug, wind leads, carry gear down the stairs,
sweat sticking shirts to backs,
load into dented white transit.

Fried egg roll from van parked outside Bethnal Green church.
Fags. Tea. Heavy sleep, limbs aching, the rich wine of the songs
still pouring through us.

Benni

Benni's a flick of hair over small ears.
Her fingers are strong, smooth knuckled,
Spread wide, they coax gruff bass strings
into strut and groove, or prance over piano keys,
sending notes skittering across the wooden floor.

Together we take tubes, steamy buses, huddle
in the leathery warmth of taxis, catch the train
to her parents' house, which is like my parents' house:
the swirly lounge carpet, the glow of the electric two-bar fire.
When we share a bath her thighs rise
creamy, smooth from the soapy water.

One evening, as I perch beside her
on a tube station bench, listening for the mournful howl
of the train barrelling down the tunnel, I remember the night
the thickset man who'd smile-waved me
through the ticket barrier
crept down the escalator and shoved his penis
through the metal grille of the bridge arching over the lines.

I stumbled away up the platform longing for
another traveller to appear.

But I don't
tell her this, not wanting to break the atmosphere
hovering between us like a feather.

Ruthie

Beautiful one, do you remember that train journey
into the hills? You opened the tall pages
of your book and as the wheels rattled we searched
for the right words to describe ourselves – ones
that didn't simper or blush, but stood bare
as stone is bare, with no need of adornment.

I loved the loops of your handwriting, forested
with crossings-out, adjustments. I wanted
to shelter in their ovals and circles, their curves.
How full of longing we were – clouds about to burst.
Oh, we knew about making love. Our bodies had been breached.
We'd shared morning cups of tea and roll-ups with lovers.

But we wanted to be seen, to be heard, and our bed-fellows
were forever looking the other way, or down at themselves.

13

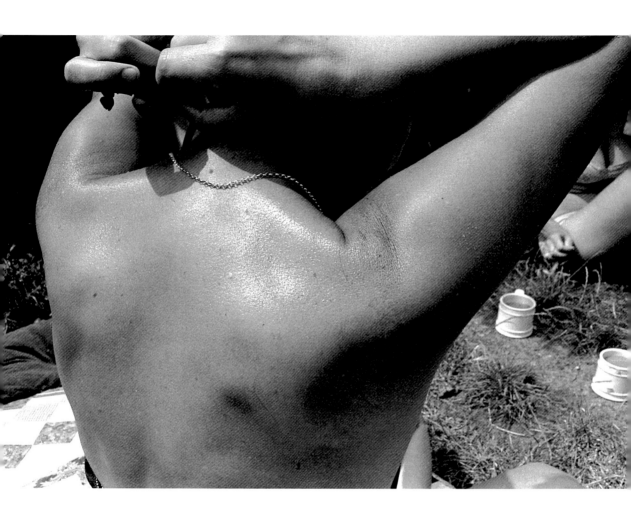

The Teacher

Weekdays I pull on the purple paisley tunic
sewn by my mother and head for school,
where I risk my job by answering any question
lobbed my way: *Miss? What do homosexuals do?*
What's oral sex? Teaching drama, I turn the girls
into tigers, tempests, rebels and birds.

Weeknights I excavate the sweet spot
in the middle of a beat and with my Sisters
lay down vocals secure as handshakes. Later,
my busy mouth disputes, protests. Songs and poems
rain on to my spiral notebooks, forming splashes, splodges.

And on summer weekends I strip off my clothes
and naked as a leaf offer my body to the Stepney sun.
My heart's a well-oiled engine, ticking over
in a garden smelling of grass mown in the nearby park,
only missing a beat now and then.

Nony

Nony fronts out the bailiffs,
brandishing the Bill of Rights 1689.
She's unfazed by trashed toilet bowls,
missing mains fuses, bashed up banisters,
Hand her the tools and she'll hang a door,
unpick a lock, unblock a drain.

Watch her stride into the dimlit saloons
of the DHSS like a gunslinger
with both hands on her Colt 45s.
And, yes, she strolls out, Stetson
pushed back from her good, honest face,
with the bounty due to her, humming.

Susy

Even when her belly's swelling,
green-eyed Susy marshals the beats
until they drive the songs
sure as a double-decker bus.

A litter of white kittens mew
in the corner of the room she's preparing
for a cot, a pram. Childless, we watch
round-eyed as she balloons.

The Van

All donkey-jacket hunch, knuckles a bunch
of fives, the fixer of the squatters union
gestures to the back of the van, says
Climb in then, ladies, and when we do it smells
manly, of roll-ups and shaving soap and tools
jumbled in the hessian bag slumped
beside the wheel arch. *Just kick that out the way*
he says and I swear the whole of Stepney is there
in his jack-the-lad mouth.

                                   Thrown around like
aggregate in a cement mixer, the three us clutch arms
and squeal as the van whips round the corner
on to the Commercial Road. Laughter runs through us
like water down a drain as we swing
through the white-shine snake of the Rotherhithe,
our sleeping bags rolling around our feet.

Stoneyard Lane Prefabs

Two ticks and the fixer of the squatters union
  has done the break-in, courtesy of a jemmy.
The door creaks in the fish-mud breeze blowing up
  from Shadwell docks. *Here you are girls.*
Faces poke, glint through curtain cracks of other prefabs.

At midnight a man comes back for his hobnailed boots.
  Stands beneath an orange street light, his meek face
breathing beer. *We got behind with the rent,* he says,
  muddy boot laces spilling over his knuckles.
Thought we'd leave before the council chucked us out.

The next morning two hoods from the council break the lock,
  bawl through the drunken door, *Clear out or we'll
board you in.* Bump-clang of an Audi brings bailiffs.
  The fixer flies in, fists up to his chin.
Has words. We hunch on the kerb with our carrier bags.

The fixers of the Squatters' Union

These men wear jeans and clean cotton shirts
that fall open on their necks as they lug a mattress
out of a flat on a Shadwell estate
where a Bengali family's had pot-shots
fired at their windows
and shit shoved through the letter-box.

When a gang of thugs sent by the council
draws up outside a block of empty flats
carrying sledgehammers, pick-axes, liquid cement,
the fixers flip over the gang's van easy as upending a chair.

They need help of the clerical kind
so, mindful of what they've done for us,
we type stencils on a flighty electric machine
so the word can be sent out to fix things
that are *a bloody disgrace*
and shouldn't be allowed.

We do what we can, and are grateful
for what they do for us and others.

27

Poplar Housing Estate 1975

This Bangladeshi family have been stuffed
into a block that butts up against the old dock wall.

A lairy man from the flats opposite
has chucked a brick through the toilet window
while the children slept. A racist, red with rage,
has aimed his airgun at the flat and shot
a ragged hole in the kitchen window pane.

When we visit, the family line up, shy,
to be photographed beside armchairs embroidered
with crowns of leaves knotted by a single flower.

York Square

We lugged sleeping bags, teapots, books,
jumpers hand-knitted by our mothers
in the narrow door of that leaning house.

We choked on the soot that flobbed out of the chimney
when we tugged off the board nailed over the fire-place.
Swept up broken glass and brick powder,
stopped up cracks with cornflake packets.

The back gardens were heaps of crot,
but we didn't go there: our senses
were drawn to the light pouring in the petals
of glass above the front door, and the city thrum
sliding through the letter box.

Tinkers

Two twelve-year old scruffs
from a family we call *tinkers*,
door-knock asking for work
so they can buy *food for the baby.*

We ask them to tidy the back garden –
a grot zone where corrugated iron sheets
groan and creak, and washing lines sag with
dark-droop tights and gorilla knickers.
A single cirrus sheet hangs
beside a pranged, upturned bed.

The boys crook-pile bricks, sort
through midden, unearth potatoes
softened to mush, rusted springs,
brillo pad boxes, tins itching
to slice open a palm. Finished,
they trample dirt into the house.

We sit them on copies of
the *Daily Mirror,* pour tea
from a pot. Rose-cheeked,
they slurp, swallow, not meeting
our eyes, long lashes cast down,
waiting for their sixty pence.

My Mother's War

One night, as I huddled in pyjamas, pullover,
hat and socks, watching a sliver of night
slide through a gap between walls, I'm sure I heard
the crash that woke you thirty years before.
I saw your eyes jerk open in your rented room
as you waited for your life to be snuffed out
only to find a bomb blast two doors up had
shaken a print of Harwich from its hook
and dashed it to the floor.

By day you counted heartbeats, doled out pills,
carried bedpans to the slop of the sluice room.
You didn't last long: a sickly swoon
washed over you like black oil when you undid
an airman's bandage seeping blood and yellow pus.
But in my leaky attic room, in that house
in the midst of bomb sites, I touched your young
bony face. Saw you fasten your nurse's cap
in the smoky dawn, blue eyes radiant with life.

Muriel: Mile End Automatic Laundry

Muriel, busy with service washes, always says hello
to the scruffs from the squats off Commercial Road –
more of them now, breaking into the slums left behind
when the GLC moved people out –
and though she doesn't stick her nose
where it's not wanted, you can tell a lot
by a person's washing, can't you?
That girl with the hacked-off hair
has no bras in her laundry bag,
and no fancy knickers.

Walking home one night she hears
music – not the jukebox, but a group
with drums, guitars, the lot – coming from
the Prince Albert. So she peeps in
and there's the girl with short hair,
in front of an all-girl group, singing
You can get it if you really want.

Muriel shakes her head. Plods home
with her heavy shopping bag, thinking,
Good for you, ducks. Good for you.

Brick Lane

Gusts of rust-red chilli leap out of
the Nazrul curry house where we feed
on Friday nights from plain white bowls,
gasping and grabbing for glasses of
thick lassi as the bhunas and jalfrezis
firebomb the soft tissues of our mouths.

On the pavement a stall laid out
on a flowered curtain sells
enamel bowls, pots and pans. Another
offers DIY tat, brass axes. We talk
in loud voices. Gobble warm beigels
stuffed with plump raisins and cinnamon.

Further up the street we come across
a wriggle of puppies, and, in a pyramid
of cages, cheeping canaries bright as lemons.
I've just left a boyfriend, having lost faith
in the frail connection that fizzed between us.
Tears spill, though we're all laughing, bumping
arm against arm. The puppies smell of spice.

41

The Muses come to our gig at North London Poly, Aldgate East

The whole gaggle wangled a lift to the gig then
wouldn't shut up. Pen in hand, Calliope urged us to
Tell it how it is. Let them know about the battles we fought.

Muscular Melpomene growled that we were too damn nice:
Show them blood and blue-black eyes.
Don't sweeten the pill, whatever you do.

Clio, prim nose buried in her scrolls, advised,
Look to your forebears. they know best. Breath
perfumed by wood, drippy Euterpe advocated a flute:
You're too rowdy and raucous. Attend to your souls.

Strumming her lyre and making cow's eyes,
Erato purred in her man-pleasing voice,
Did you have to cut out all the sweet baby talk?

Plain Polyhymnia tried to weasel her waspy drones
into our charts, muttering, *I'm more like you*
than you think. We told dreamy Urania
to wait outside: no time to stargaze.
We'd got a gig to do.

Boyish Thalia cracked jokes from the traps case.
Come on girls lighten up. Don't be so bloody glum.
Terpsichore, was our favourite – she kept her mouth
shut, grabbed her lyre and swayed her curvy hips,
ready to hit the beer-sticky dance floor
once the amps were glowing hot enough to burn.

Saxophone

This woman with a red cloud of curls
and kindness in her mouth, whose tables creak
with freesias and food, has put away her cello
and its frayed bow, mothballed its soundbox
filled with the voice of England's lush hillsides
to take up a brassy assembly of tubes, rods, levers and caps.

With eyes pinched shut she uses breath and spit
to construct the swoop and whoop, honk and hoot
of jazz and soul. Long fingers run spider fast as she
blows her notes through the fug of this no-shit pub
on the lip of a down-at-heel crescent, where locals
mutter into their pints, and the landlord, listening,
leans his elbows on the sticky bar.

                              I'm at a table,
drinking music that's like daffodils, dandelions –
everything that comes round again and again,
fuelled by giddy hope.

Moira

Big-booted, smudged with oil,
you love getting your head under a bonnet
to tame a tappet or persuade an injection pump
to behave. You dry out spark plugs in the blast
of a blow heater; coax sulky engines
to sputter and grump into life. We hover
at the door, watching as your mouth
gets within kissing distance of our van's
patched-up radiator. With a grin
you straighten the ripple of your back,
smoothing back a lick of chestnut hair.
Pronounce she'll be fit to go in an hour.

I've heard your fingers can make a woman purr
like a cat in a lap. To us you're a miracle
in mucky blue overalls. Behind the wheel
you're steady as Big Ben, coaxing the van uphill,
your green eyes watching the A12 unfold.

The Festival Inn

Fuelled up, we roared towards Vauxhall, and like
the corseted revellers who slid into corners of
the Foxhall Pleasure Gardens behind wet quivers
of leaves, and kissed until their boot soles
sank into the mud, we hid bottles under our cloaks,
hitched our hems, and danced until *The Way I Want to Touch you*
poured through us like milk through muslin, until the city
dissolved into atoms, less than atoms, and all that existed was
the push of breasts against breasts, the tang of Eau Sauvage.

No one grabbed our arses or called us slags. No one
spiked our drinks or tried to fuck us when we were
comatose. We rode back, heads lolling, until our driver
turfed us out in front of loose-jointed houses. Spreadeagled,
loosened by dancing, we slept on second-hand beds, safe.

The Letter

One morning I received a letter from a woman
splashed with the words *beautiful* and *cunt.*

I took the letter to the school where I taught, wanting to feel
its pulse in my pocket. Dropped it on the walk home. Heart
tumbling like a discarded crisp packet I criss-crossed
the route to and from school, scouring gutters and puddles.

An elderly colleague, unmarried and possibly gay,
found it nearby with a muddy footprint dirtying the blue ink.
In the stifling staff room he handed it back the next day:
Here: I thought you'd like to have this.

                                Later, I lay
naked on my bed, watching my heart push at the skin
of my ribs, waiting for the red telephone to ring,
realising the blossoms of the horse chestnut tree
had opened while I wasn't looking.

Sunday Morning Market

Earth is tipping towards noon and I'm drowsy
and dusty-toed, watching your long fingers
scuffle piles of biros, batteries, drawing-pins,
staples – you love this sort of gumph – head
dipping forward so your hair parts like water
on the pale stem of your neck. From my wrist
dangles a bag of oranges, smelling of Seville.

When our thumbs brush my cells scatter
leaving me full of nothing until your mouth wings
down, bringing breath, a sealing kiss. You steer me,
your palm a sun in the small of my back,
to fried-egg rolls, golden-full and yielding.

Street Sweepers

Council-issue donkey jackets slung over saggy suits,
      the street sweepers get to work,
broom heads shooshing over concrete and tar,
      herding paper, peel and fag ends into heaps,

strong fingers grasping the broom handles,
      knuckles big and smooth as weathered stones
moving easy in their bags of skin, watchful eyes
      on you, your button-clicks, your lens.

Clippie

Those women's libbers are marching again,
stopping the bus with their placards and banners,
their shouts and chants, and this clippie
with a silver ticket machine slung round her neck
is squizzing the leaflet shoved into her hand.

Not that she minds: it gives her a break
from swinging up and down the stairs,
or swaying along the aisles, looking for
the pond life staring out of the window,
pretending they've paid when they haven't.

Look at her now, lush as a butter caramel,
sleeves rolled up and pockets sagging.
Who shoved the leaflet into her palm?
And what do the words say? It might yell
Murderers ... Butchers ... Baby killers.
Or it could chant *Rights ... Women ... Choose*

A Police Officer protects Mothercare

When this officer asked the super
why they weren't at Millwall, it being
a home-match Saturday and the stands
rammed with grade-A louts, the super
scrunched his eyebrows and said:
Women's Lib. Guard the doors

as if they were to expect a stampede
of shrieking banshees to
rip up maternity dresses
instead of this motley bunch
singing daft songs about sisterhood
as they stroll past.

Meanwhile the officer's sweating
in tickly serge, trying not to
think about when the missus
does her *consciousness raising*
yakking nineteen to the dozen with
a bunch of wives from up the road,
leaving the ironing in a heap
and the pots and pans in the sink.

Tower of Righteousness

When we sweep into Trafalgar Square, here they are –
these young bloods with straight-chopped fringes
and chunky sideburns
composing and recomposing
        their tableaux
beneath the coil of Nelson's rope.

Blink and they could be revolutionaries
        stacking themselves up behind Danton
in the Place d'Etoile,

but these firebrands are shaking stiff placards
hammered to wood
instead of flags swishing like horses' tails

and though their heads of hair are apple-scented
and their tank-tops and Bolan flares cut a dash
        their mouths are ruled straight and

their words, written in stark capitals,
are acid drops you wouldn't want to suck.

Notting Hill Carnival

I took the bus, riding the smoky top deck
from the kung fu palace and raucous boozers of the east
to the flat-fronts of the west. Round their scruffed bricks
bodies eddied, pulsed, powered by beats rumbling out of
speakers stacked under the grumble of the Westway.

The smells of the market hung in the air:
bruise-bloomed mangoes, yellowing cabbages,
the neon-squish scent of discarded satsumas.

My whole body swayed when I breathed in
the husky burr of dope and coconut oil on plaits.
I slipped through the crowds, bumping up against
swishing skirts knotted at the waist with sashes,
tidy suits and glossy neck-ties. I felt the scorch
of a dude with a cream fedora propped slant-wise
on a close-clipped head.

In the cool shadow of the underpass I let
Rock Your Baby fill me up like a milk bottle
until the cream settled at the top of my head.

As dusk swallowed me up, a man kissed sweet beer
into me until I couldn't walk a straight line.
For those ten minutes I loved that man, loved
his mouth, loved the city where we didn't need
to lock ourselves, our beating hearts,
into small, separate boxes.

The West London Writing Group

On Wednesday evenings, full of tea and baked beans on toast,
I wrapped my scarf round my neck – a soft, animal thing,

flecked in amber and brown, the colour of my dog back home –
dragged my moped on to the road, kicked the pedal. Kicked it

again. Again. When it finally started I puttered past the library
in the Nissan hut that smelled of mushrooms, buzzed through the city,

and on to the Marylebone Road, passing the Royal Academy of Music,
climbing on to the Westway, a grimy lift of tarmac that let me peep into

kitchen windows and see women at the sink or the cooker. I savoured
the tweed of streets, lush gardens, slates, tiles, chimneys

coughing coal smoke. I turned off at Westbourne Grove into
streets with tall, tattered houses until I reached the room where women

threw words into the ring like punches. The youngest, and English,
I drank down their stories of samovars and sophomores,

rolling the glitz of New York round my palate.
Four hours later, weaving home, words spilled from my head,

leaving an alphabet trail behind me, a poem in motion.

Women's Free Arts Alliance Exhibition 1975

Look: a squished-up line of kitchen utensils
wonky as bunioned feet
with the instruction
Please play these with a wooden spoon

Let me praise women tied into aprons in sweltering kitchens
who made cheese on toast
with a smear of fiery mustard,
and boiled up the lava of sticky strawberry jam tarts.

Listen hard and you'll hear the clack-clack
of their knives chopping cabbage in colanders or
the whir-whir shoosh of whisks
seeding froth in evaporated milk to make it go further.

Mums, aunties, grannies, family friends
squeezed into dresses too small for their busts:
know that we struck and shook and rattled your utensils
till their metal clatter
ran down the stairs and through old-gent London streets
whose facades were in need of a stitch and a polish.

Can you hear our blows, our hoo-hah,
as you lean towards two-bar electric fires,
knitting lumpy jumpers for girls who couldn't settle at home
like tabbies by the fire
but instead are prowling round London, caterwauling?

Eviction

January has sauntered over the hill, leaving
draggle and bone-cold in its wake, when
the GLC man knocks on our door, extracting
our names easy as shelling peas. And he's
civil, verging on kind, with a spud face
and a flop of grey hair, inscribing
our names in careful, royal-blue script.
As he clicks the cap on his fountain pen
he offers: *Six weeks before you have to go.*

On a foul February day we all squidge
into the dock of Bow County Court, shoving
to the front our very own Portia who claims
We're socially indispensable. Biting back
his smile, the wizened judge pronounces:
In legal terms the case is cut and dried.
Possession order granted to the GLC.

Afterwards we plod home glum as children
in detention. Within a month the house
is stripped of the music carried in our mouths
from Detroit and New York, but passing it one day
when rain's tottering from its coat of scaffolding
I swear I hear the plaintive breath of our voices
tapping at the window cracks: *R-E-S-P-E-C-T.*

They Changed the World

Let me praise those sisters bundled into creaky houses
who could Sassoon a thicket of hair with a bent brush
and a fan heater, wire up the cassette recorder
to a two-pin plug socket, and swallow a friend's rant
about bloody men like a buttery crumpet.

Nightly, they returned to raggedy nests dragging
curtain poles, a kitchen table, cooker cable, drum sticks,
mars bars, guitar strings. One bell-rung Sunday
they jiggled a mattress in the jaws of the tube train doors
and floated it home on their heads. Nightly, over plates
of vegetable crumble they swapped tales
of high-strung prancers, wriggle-hip chancers,
underground wankers, cervix watchers, council nasties.

They sat in the outside toilet watching spiders
weave their webs amid the scents
of crushed grass and run-wild mint,
and boiled five kettles and a saucepan to fill a tin bath

They were beer swillers, women's libbers,
bolshie sheilas, good, industrious worker bees.

They changed the world.
Praise them.

The Stepney Sisters

Ruthie Smith and Caroline Gilfillan

Nony Ardill

Benni Lees

Susy Hogarth

Notes on the photographs

p.2 Upper photo: **Bromley Street, Stepney, summer 1975**

Most of the houses had been bricked shut by the landlord, the Greater London Council (GLC). There were a few places that had not been sealed and all were squatted. All the houses in the street have now been renovated and let to tenants. AS

p.2 Lower photo: **view from the rear of a squatted house, Bromley Street, of squatted houses in Westport Street, Stepney, spring 1975**

p.5 **Caroline, Bromley Street squat, Stepney, July 1976**

During my teenage years I'd happily embraced false eyelashes and pink lipstick, but in the heady days of Women's Liberation, I gave up on make-up. And I've got a feeling I cut my hair myself, with nail scissors. It was liberating to let go of all the effort that went into looking like a 'proper woman'. CG

p.6 **Stepney Sisters, meeting, Westport Street squat, Stepney, summer 1975**

Late in 1974, when we'd moved into Stepney squats, we started to sing and play music in the evenings, beginning with soul music classics we'd learned as part of a soul band while at university. The backing vocals of *Respect* by Aretha Franklin echoed round fuggy rooms warmed by paraffin heaters. Then we turned our hands to writing original songs which reflected our lives and concerns. We learned instruments so we could play the songs as well as sing them. By early 1975 we'd formed a women's band called the Stepney Sisters. (See the poem *We formed a band.*) We did a couple of gigs and were offered many more. This was a time when women were examining their roles, their words and actions, and so the band had regular meetings to discuss which gigs to accept, how to dress, how to promote ourselves, and how to develop the music. It's fair to say that these meetings were hard work, but they were also stimulating, empowering. Having said, that, we heaved a collective sigh of relief when they were over. CG

The building on the top left is the old market building, still a fruit, veg and flower market in the 1970s. I was a member of a small fruit and veg collective set up by a group of squatters. We all took turns to get to Spitalfields market by 6 am on a Saturday, I think, with orders from members of the community to buy fruit and veg. The produce was generally very good and cheap, wholesale prices. On one occasion a stall holder, white, male, middle aged, asked me what the courgettes and aubergines I'd just bought from him were like to eat! We were living in a world in which these modern staples were considered exotic and alien. AS

Yes folks, back in the olden days all double deck London buses had conductors or conductresses who sold you your ticket, gave the driver the signal to drive away from each bus stop and generally kept order. Clippie was the widely used nickname for conductresses, although why this word came into use isn't clear, nor why it only applied to conductresses. AS

Notes on the poems

p.8 Gig

This was a time when live music flourished. The legislation that prevented venues from putting on bands larger than a duo without a specific licence was in the distant future. Our gigs were a mixture of pubs, benefits, women's events and festivals. Speakers in those days were huge beasts, but we lugged them up and down flights of stairs, plugged in and let rip. CG

p.15 The Teacher

I'd found a job teaching English and Drama at Highbury High School for Girls. There was much I loved about the job, though I did seem to have a dual life, as a teacher by day, and a radical feminist in a women's band by night. As the poem states, I was willing to answer all the questions about sex that were thrown at me by students who received no teaching about reproduction or sex. Such frank answers could have got me sacked – but didn't. CG

p.16 Nony

Nony Ardill, guitarist with The Stepney Sisters, worked in the field of social justice all her life, and after training as a solicitor became a leading human rights lawyer. Always knowledgeable about legal rights, she was a formidable advocate even in those early days. She died in April 2021, and is much missed. CG

p.24 The fixers of the Squatters' Union

The local Squatters' Union was run by a number of highly principled, practical men, keen to put right some of the housing injustices that were staring us all in the face. Much of their work was concerned with Bangladeshi families, as Andrew Scott explains in one of his notes, but they were also kind to waifs and strays like us, helping us to find somewhere to live, for a while at least. CG

p.32 **York Square and Tinkers**

Stepney was far from the gentrified enclave it's become in recent years. Our new house had an outside toilet (which didn't bother us at all), no bathroom (we got used to washing using bowls and buckets) and back gardens filled with rubble and rubbish. We were happy there. The fact that we referred to our neighbours as 'tinkers' shows how unaware we were of the racist connotations of the label. CG

p.35 **My Mother's War**

In my York Square bedroom, there was a visible gap between the side and back walls, possibly caused by a bomb blast during the Second World War. Huddled in that bedroom at night, I felt spiritually connected to my mother, who'd spent time in London during WW2. One night I'm sure her younger self visited me. CG

p.46 **Moira**

At this time women were entering trades usually occupied by men. A number took motor mechanic courses, learning how to keep their vehicles on the road, and sometimes transporting us and our gear to gigs. CG

p.68 **The West London Writing Group**

In 1975 I joined a women's writing group in West London, and wrote my first poems. It was a thrilling experience, starting me on a writing career I've continued until this day. CG

p.69 **Women's Free Arts Alliance Exhibition 1975**

The Stepney Sisters played their first gig at the Women's Free Arts Alliance, Chalk Farm, on 14 February 1975 at an exhibition titled *Sweet Sixteen and Never Been Shown*. Benni, our bass player, created an installation of household implements which people could touch, rattle or bang as they entered the gallery. CG

Biographies

Caroline Gilfillan has published four collections of poetry, and her work has appeared in many anthologies and journals, including *Poetry News* and *Mslexia*. Her collection *Yes*, won the best poetry book prize in the East Anglian Book Awards. She won the Yeovil Poetry Prize in 2019, and was a runner-up in in the Edward Thomas prize 2021. She's also written two crime novels, *The Terrace*, and *The Peasmarsh Players*. After playing with The Stepney Sisters, she performed with  other women-only bands, including Sisterhood of Spit, Hi Jinx, The Ponytails and Crikey Aphrodite. A songwriter, she now performs with Debs Williams in the duo Further to Fly in the Lake District, where she lives.

Andrew Scott is a photographer, living in London. His dad taught him the basics and for the rest he is self-taught. His work has appeared in the Whitechapel Gallery, Photofusion, Lounge and Photo Open in London and the *Daily Telegraph* and *Spitalfields Life* online. His photographs of the East End have been archived by the Bishopsgate Institute in London. *Hail Sisters*, with his dear friend Caroline Gilfillan, is his first publication.

Acknowledgements

From Caroline Gilfillan

These poems could not have been written without the encouragement of the other Stepney Sisters, especially Nony Ardill, who was a cheerleader from when the book was first conceived. I am grateful to Kim Moore, who gave invaluable advice on the first draft of the collection, and to Jennifer Copley, who helped me to develop and redraft the poems over many sessions in her garden. I'm also grateful to the members of Brewery Poets and Fourth Monday Poets, who gave helpful feedback on drafts. Finally, I offer huge thanks for Andrew Scott, who created the book with me and provided his extraordinary photographs, and Russell Holden at Pixel Tweaks, who provided design skills and technical expertise.

A version of Women's Free Arts Alliance Exhibition 1975 appeared in *Reflected Light* (Grey Hen Press, 2020).

From Andrew Scott

Big thankyous to Rocío Vázquez Landázuri for insight, conversations, laughs and love.